THE SECRET ART OF BEING A PARENT

THE SECRET ART OF BEING A PARENT

TIPS, TRICKS, and LIFESAVERS YOU DON'T HAVE to LEARN the HARD WAY

BRIDGET WATSON PAYNE
Illustrations by Rachel Harrell

CHRONICLE BOOKS
SAN FRANCISCO

Library of Congress Cataloging-in-Publication Data:

Names: Payne, Bridget Watson, author.

Title: The secret art of being a parent / Bridget Watson Payne.

Description: San Francisco : Chronicle Books, [2019]

Identifiers: LCCN 2018013780 | ISBN 9781452171227 (hardcover : alk. paper)

Subjects: LCSH: Parenting. | Child rearing.

Classification: LCC HQ755.8 .P39929 2019 | DDC 306.874—dc23 LC record
available at https://lccn.loc.gov/2018013780

Manufactured in China

Design by **Rachel Harrell**

10 9 8 7 6 5 4 3 2 1

Chronicle books and gifts are available at special quantity discounts to corpora-
tions, professional associations, literacy programs, and other organizations. For
details and discount information, please contact our corporate/premiums depart-
ment at corporatesales@chroniclebooks.com or at 1-800-759-0190.

Chronicle Books LLC
680 Second Street
San Francisco, California 94107
www.chroniclebooks.com

To parents everywhere:
you've *so* got this.

Hello, parent!

OR SOON-TO-BE-PARENT! WELCOME TO THIS BOOK!

When you're going to become a parent, or have recently become one, the world and the people around you suddenly become extremely determined to tell you two very big, important, and seemingly contradictory things.

On the one hand, they want you to know that this is going to be the most amazing, wonderful, joyful, transcendent thing you ever have done or ever will do in your life.

On the other hand, they want to be sure to let you know that this is going to suck eggs in the most exhausting, overwhelming, daunting, confusing way you've ever experienced.

And you're just like: Wait, what? Huh? Make up your minds, people! Which is it!?

And the secret is: it's both. And the even bigger secret is: it's neither.

Yes, being a parent alters your whole reality. Yes, your life will never be the same again. And yes, you will experience pure, unadulterated joy—the beating-heart magic of life itself. And yes, you will experience bone-deep exhaustion—along with some of the most exquisite annoyances ever known to humankind.

But here's the thing: It will also just be life. Your life. Going along the way life does. Only now with a very prominent and very small new cast member.

And all those other parents are so busy predicting how the heavens will part the first time you see your child, or how you'll want to tear out your own hair from sleep deprivation two weeks in, that they forget to tell you the really important stuff.

The good stuff. The *useful* stuff.

All the tips, tricks, and perks (yes, perks!) of parenthood that they figured out for themselves as they went along. All the knowledge parents use in their actual, real, day-to-day lives.

It's not their fault. It's just that this stuff becomes so ingrained, completely second nature, that pretty soon, parents forget there was a time they ever didn't know it. But no one is born knowing how to pack a diaper bag (page 48), or how to fly on a plane with a child (page 72), or how to harness baby laughter as a natural mood elevator (page 60).

Which is where this book comes in. Practical smarts, emotional know-how, logistics and expectations, time-savers and support. Rather than reinvent the wheel, here is a cheat sheet of the stuff it usually takes parents years to figure out.

This is going to be fun, and you're going to do great. Seriously. You've got this.

The secret to being home with an infant:

When they nap, you nap.

Forget the dishes or the thank-you notes or whatever else you think you ought to be doing. If you are tired (and you will be), then the minute that baby conks out, you go lie down on your bed too.

Get your z's when you can!

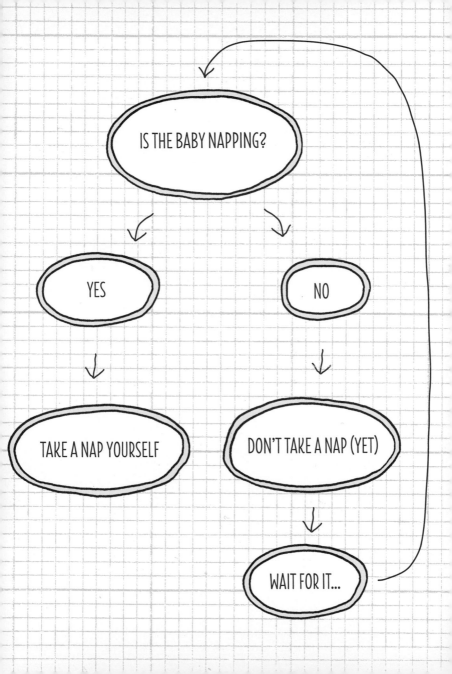

What to do if you drop the pacifier on the ground somewhere out in the world where you can't rinse it off:

Pop the pacifier in your own mouth.

SUCK ON IT FOR A MINUTE, THEN GIVE IT BACK TO YOUR CHILD.

 EW, RIGHT?

Yeah, but here's the thing:

Your adult immune system can most likely handle the germs from the ground (think of how many times in your adult life you've invoked the five-second rule with no ill effects).

And:

Your baby is already accustomed to dealing with all your germs from being around you all the time (think of how many times you've kissed said baby with that same mouth).

Problem solved.

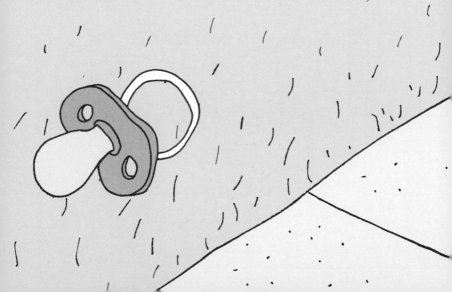

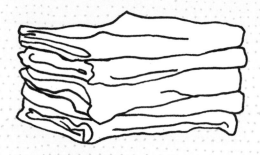

Diaper changing is messy. Actively messy. For some reason folks tend to imply that this is only the case with boys, but girl babies are just as capable of wreaking changing-table havoc in all directions.

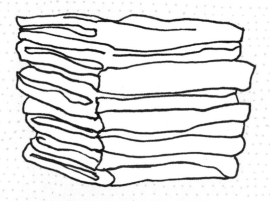

When changing the baby, always keep a diaper cloth draped over your shoulder.

FOR CONTENDING WITH THE UNEXPECTED MESSES THAT WILL INEVITABLY OCCUR NOW AND THEN.

You do not need a baby bathtub.

THAT'S WHAT KITCHEN SINKS ARE FOR.

One less thing to spend money on, one less thing to clutter up your life. And, if nothing else, just think of the photo op!

Babies in sinks = most adorable pics ever.

If you're worried about the hardness and slipperiness of the sink, you can always line it with a nice thick towel.

The 1st year of your baby's life is the longest and the shortest year of yours.

This is what people are talking about when they say "the days are long but the years are short"—which is such a bafflingly phrased cliché that, until you experience it for yourself, it's pretty much incomprehensible.

But it turns out there's a reason why sentiments like that one, and "they grow up so fast," are clichés. They've become well-worn phrases because billions of parents have said them. And billions of parents have said them because they are true.

An afternoon spent at home with a baby can feel like the slowest, lengthiest afternoon you've ever spent anywhere with anyone in your life.

Things your baby does—especially things that worry or concern you—like not sleep through the night, for instance, or cry when anyone but you holds them, seem to go on and on, and feel as if they will continue to go on and on, forever.

And yet the year will also have a blink-and-you'll-miss-it quality. Hard as it is to believe, before you know it you'll be throwing a first birthday party.

Someone will ask you what age your child was when they stopped doing some particular thing—drooling, for example, or spitting up—and you'll suddenly realize you have no idea. Something that, at one point, was a seemingly eternal part of your everyday reality will have disappeared without you even noticing. They grew out of it.

Time, which seemed not to be passing at all, passed.

The secret to an equal division of labor between mothers and fathers forever:

Both parents need time to be the main baby-minder, alone, while the baby is still tiny.

Studies show that when each parent has time to take care of the baby on their own early on, the partnership becomes more equitable. A happy family is one in which not only childcare but also housework and other domestic tasks are shared more evenly. The baby doesn't become the mom's exclusive domain, and traditional gender roles are not defaulted to.

IN A PERFECT WORLD THIS TAKES THE FORM OF PATERNITY LEAVE. BUT WHEN THAT'S NOT AVAILABLE, THERE ARE OTHER OPTIONS:

- Take a week—or even just a few days—of vacation time to stay home alone with the baby.

- Send one parent away with friends each Saturday so the other parent gets time on their own with the kiddo.

- Mom signs up for an evening class or makes a standing weeknight commitment, and Dad handles bath time and bedtime.

This applies just as much to same-sex couples or families with stay-at-home dads. Solo parenting time for both partners is the key.

Read to your kid A LOT.

Here's a secret:

When they're an infant, you can even read them your own book or magazine or newspaper or whatever you'd like to be reading yourself.

THEY JUST LIKE HEARING YOUR VOICE.

There is no magic wand.

When you're wracking your brain trying to figure out what caused your baby to do or not do this or that thing (sleep, not sleep, poop, not poop, spit up a lot, etc.) and you find yourself thinking, "Maybe it was because I fed them that apricot?"

The answer is: No, it wasn't the apricot.

Cause and effect is not that direct or literal when it comes to babies.

 THEY JUST DO WHAT THEY DO.

This is both alarming and soothing.

On the one hand it means:

THERE IS NO EASY FIX TO YOUR PROBLEM.

But on the other hand:

IT'S NOT YOUR FAULT.

Hint: NOT something you'd find in a baby's room

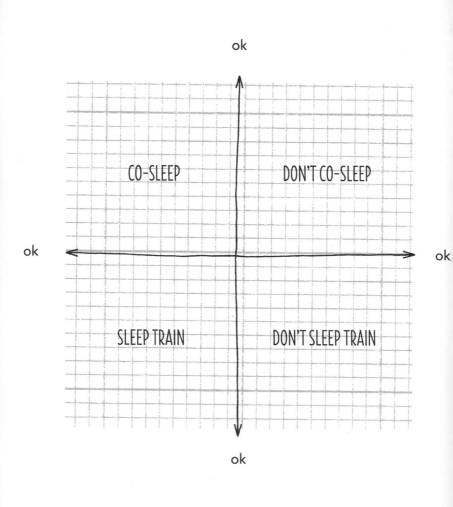

Regarding sleep:

Do what is best for you and your family.

DON'T LET ANYONE GIVE YOU ANY GUFF ABOUT IT.

Of course, they will anyway.

But you can ignore them.

Same goes for decisions regarding whether to breastfeed or not and for how long. It's nobody's business but your own. Other people's baggage is not your problem.

Studies show that the current generation of parents spends more time with their children—and specifically more time actively parenting their children (that is, actually engaging with the kids, as opposed to just being in the same room with them but doing separate things)—than any previous generation of parents ever has since scientists started studying and measuring this stuff.

And yet, we also feel guiltier about not spending enough time with our kids than any previous generation has ever felt since scientists started studying and measuring parental guilt.

This is a double bind of almost staggering proportions. If more-time-parenting-than-any-previous-modern-generation-ever is still not enough, what will ever be? Nothing.

Like all guilt traps, the only way out of this one is to release yourself from its unreasonable terms. There was no idyllic time in the past when parents were better parents than we are now. Parents are just parents are just parents.

THE UPSHOT IS:

You are doing a good job.

LET'S REPEAT THAT, SHALL WE?

You are doing a good job.

broken arm

≠

traumatized for life

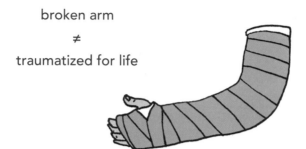

soap in eyes

≠

will hate you forever

locked out of house

≠

end of the world

One day something will go wrong.

They'll roll off the changing table, or you'll cut their tiny finger while trying to trim their nails, or you'll get all the way across town before realizing you don't have any diapers.

DON'T BEAT YOURSELF UP.

This will be easier said than done. But seriously. Everyone's parents screwed up at some point and we all turned out just fine. Your kid will too.

You are 100% entitled to breastfeed in public.

NO IFS, ANDS, OR BUTS.*

This isn't just a warm, fuzzy sentiment—you are in fact legally protected in a wide variety of circumstances. Familiarize yourself with your rights.

Breastfeeding paraphernalia—what you do and do not need:

Stuff you need

- Nursing bra
- Nursing pads

Nursing pads are essential, and you need them from about day two. No one tells you this. Bring some with you to the hospital! And you need them at night, too, so make sure your bra is comfortable enough to sleep in, whether it's marketed as a special sleeping bra or not.

Stuff you might need

- Nursing shirts
- A pillow (from your bed)
- Rocking chair
- Nipple cream

By all means, if you want and can afford any of this stuff, that's entirely your business, but don't let anyone tell you that you have to have some particular special gimmick.

Stuff you do not need

- Giant donut-shaped nursing pillow
- Strap-on wedge-of-foam nursing pillow
- Nursing scarf
- Nursing wrap
- Nursing shawl
- Nursing poncho

There is absolutely no point in comparing your baby to anyone else's baby—not with those height and weight percentiles the pediatrician tells you about, or with what other parents report to you about their kids at the playground.

THERE IS NO ONE RIGHT WAY TO BE A BABY.

- Sleeps long stretches

- Eats a little

- Few naps

- Nurses with ease

- Slender

- Often grumpy

- Social

Every baby is different.

- Wakes up frequently
- Eats a lot
- Many naps
- Has challenges nursing
- Chubby
- Often happy
- Clingy

GOOD BABIES

Just like there's no one right way to be a baby,

there's no one right way to be a parent.

Starting well before your baby is born, and continuing on for the rest of your life, you will see other parents do things you would never do in a million years.* Things that strike you as misguided or unhealthy or just plain silly.

But think about it. If the shoe were on the other foot—and it for sure will be, frequently—would you enjoy other parents looking askance at how you choose to raise your child? Nope. You sure would not.

What's right for them may not be right for you, and vice versa. It's not your job to judge. It's your job to raise your own kid the best way you know how.

A nice flip side to this:

You don't have to live up to other people's expectations either!

Don't judge other parents.

Don't judge other parents.

Don't judge other parents.

Don't judge other parents.

Don't judge other parents.

Don't judge other parents.

Don't judge other parents.

Don't judge other parents.

Don't judge other parents.

Don't judge other parents.

Don't judge other parents.

*Obviously, if you encounter actual child abuse, all of this is moot. Judge with impunity and contact the authorities immediately.

Tips for dealing with sleep deprivation:

MOM

ENERGY

CAFFEINE.

You are wonderful,
You are loved

There is zero shame in postpartum depression.

IF YOUR ANKLE WAS DOING SOMETHING WEIRD AND PAINFUL YOU'D GET IT TREATED. SAME GOES FOR YOUR BRAIN.

If you even suspect that something is going on for you psychologically or emotionally, call your doctor immediately. If, god forbid, that doctor doesn't take you seriously right away, get help from a loved one finding a doctor who will.

Infants are easily entertained.

HOW TO ENTERTAIN A BABY:

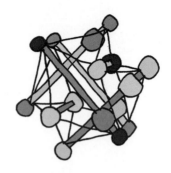

1) Spread baby blanket out on rug.

2) Place baby and one toy on blanket.

3) Lie down on rug next to baby.

4) Chat, sing, tickle, coo, wave the toy around.

Hours of entertainment!

But, pro tip: Don't blow bubbles in the baby's face. It will entertain them wonderfully for about half a minute, until soap gets in their eyes and they scream for half an hour.

The days go by in a blur.

IT'S TRULY IMPOSSIBLE TO TAKE TOO MANY PHOTOS OR VIDEOS. YOU WILL WANT THEM LATER!

However, it is possible to overshare on social media.

Even before your baby is born, think about—and talk with your partner about—how much you want to share online.

That way you can avoid retroactive remorse over either:

a) sharing more of your kid's life than you ultimately feel comfortable with, or

b) driving your friends and family up the wall with your fafillions of baby pictures.

A good and simple rule of thumb here is:

SHARE THE VERY BEST AND KEEP THE REST FOR YOURSELF.

Things to make up

USE YOUR IMAGINATION

Songs

(the songs you make up now
will warm your heart for years
to come)

←

Things not to make up

Stories

(making up stories is *hard*, just read them from books)

The answer to the question "why is the sky blue?"

(fact or fiction, they'll never check, either way you're fine)

How to pack a diaper bag

YOU FOR SURE NEED SOME STUFF, BUT YOU DO NOT NEED ALL THE STUFF.

Here's what to put in the bag*:

- Four diapers

- Small pack of wipes

- Burp cloth

- Change of clothes (onesie, pants, socks, outer layer)

- Small lightweight toy

- The right amount of dry formula in a bottle, if you're going that route

- Your keys

- Your wallet

- Your phone

- Small bottle of water

Later on, when baby starts eating people food, add:

- A snack

(Always, always, always have snacks.)

Everything else is just extra weight to lug around. And baby is heavy enough already without that.

*A note about the bag itself: Messenger-style bags are great most of the time, but if you're toting baby in a carrier where they rest on your chest, a cross-body strap is not going to work—choose a backpack instead.

If you used to be a punctual person before you had a baby, you won't be anymore.

If you used to usually run a little bit late, you will now run very late.

That's just the way it is with a baby. There's no point stressing about it. It doesn't last forever.

Getting out of the house will take way, way longer than you think it should, or ever did before.

Do yourself a favor and restock anything you used from the diaper bag as soon as you walk back into the house—that way, there's one less thing to do when you're trying to leave next time.

WHATEVER IT IS YOU'RE SUPPOSED TO BE DOING WITH
YOUR NEWBORN...

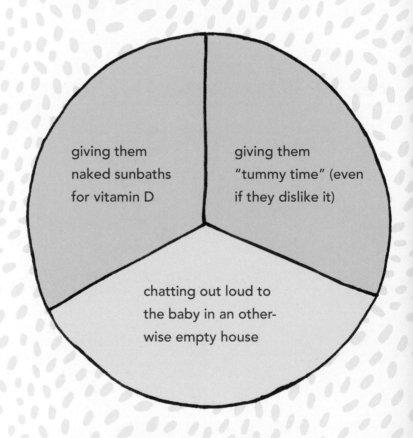

HOWEVER MUCH OF IT YOU'RE DOING…

You're doing just fine.

Let's repeat that one:

**You.
Are.
Doing.
Just.
Fine.**

Take care of yourself first so you can take care of others next.

THIS IS BASIC COMMON SENSE, BUT YOU'D BE AMAZED AT HOW OFTEN WE AS PARENTS TEND TO FORGET IT.

Of course, it's a given that, during the first year especially, you'll have to push through sleep deprivation and other assorted challenges.

But if, in the long term, you're not getting enough rest, if you're constantly on the verge of getting sick, if your work/life balance is shot to heck, if you find yourself perpetually cranky with your child or your partner, then something is going on that could use some adjusting.

Being a parent is not being a martyr. You, too, are entitled to being taken good care of—both by others and by your very own self.

It's like flight attendants say:

PUT YOUR OWN OXYGEN MASK ON FIRST BEFORE OFFERING ASSISTANCE TO OTHERS.

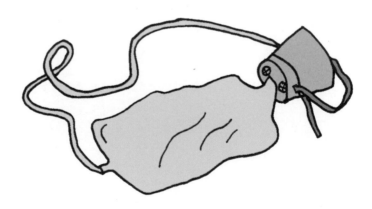

Grandparents' job is to give unconditional love and adoration to their grandkids.

(Won't it be fun when you get to do the grandparent job one day?)

You don't have to agree with the grandparents about everything.

Some of the choices you make may seem newfangled and silly to them.

But you are the boss.

Your job is to figure out how best to raise your kid.

And you are well within the bounds of what's reasonable to expect grandparents to abide by the choices you've made.

And they are well within the bounds of what's reasonable to expect you to let them bend the rules, particularly when it comes to sugary treats, now and then.

Let them do their job and you do yours.

Try out different baby carriers before you buy one.

What's comfortable for one person might not be for another. Find a friend with a baby who owns a few different models of carrier (more common than you might think) and ask if you can try them out, ideally borrowing their baby to stick in there as well. Or, some friendly baby shops will let you try them on in the store. (Again, if you can find a baby to do this with, all the better.)

Related: Don't take a stroller on the bus. Though you technically can, you'll regret it. Riding public transportation is a great time to use the carrier.

And carriers are also handy for getting stuff done around the house.

Inward-facing carrier

Front-facing carrier

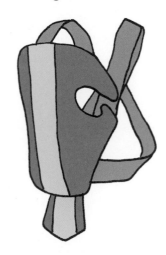

one-shoulder sling carrier

fabric wrap carrier

As your baby gets bigger, be sure to take advantage of the magical mood-lifting properties of baby laughter.

Keep an eye out for the things that fill your baby with glee.

That might be:

- mashed bananas

- peek-a-boo

- a certain black-and-white stuffed bear

- a particular song you sing

- a silly voice your partner does

- making raspberry noises

- a simple word or phrase you utter that the baby finds hilarious for secret reasons of their own

THEN, WHEN YOU FEEL OVERWHELMED OR NEED CHEERING UP:

PRODUCE THAT THING,

LISTEN TO YOUR BABY LAUGH, AND

feel your mood instantly elevate by 1,000%.

Avoid being matronizing to dads you may encounter.

Yep, matronizing. We all know what patronizing is, right? And how super-duper annoying it is? (Dads, it should go without saying: Avoid being patronizing at all costs).

Well, sometimes mothers, when they come across dads taking solo care of their children (particularly if those children are daughters), can find themselves doing a similar thing, which we will call matronizing.

That dad with his little girl at the park?

HE KNOWS HOW TO CHANGE HER DIAPER AND HOW TO DO HER HAIR.

Don't assume he doesn't. And don't be amazed that he does. Don't treat him any differently from how you treat other moms.

Meal planning will save your bacon.

Without getting overly proscriptive here—every family is different in how they choose to divide up the labor of getting the shopping and the cooking done, and so they should be*—the power of the simple act of meal planning to improve and simplify your life with children can hardly be overstated. Fewer decisions to make, less scrambling, full tummies, everyone happy.

*Remember the golden rule of being a parent: Do what's right for you and your family!

HOW TO MEAL PLAN IN THREE SIMPLE STEPS:

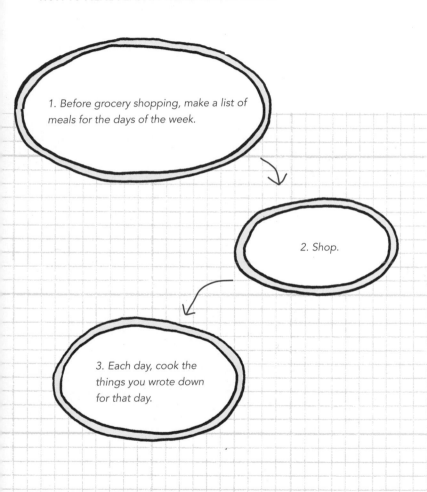

1. Before grocery shopping, make a list of meals for the days of the week.

2. Shop.

3. Each day, cook the things you wrote down for that day.

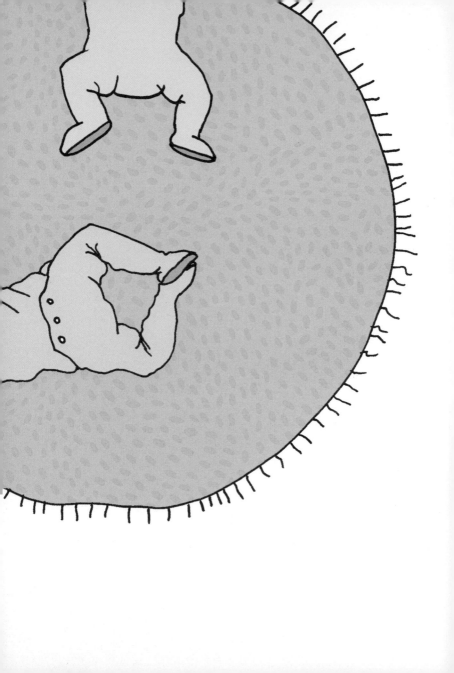

Make a baby date.

INVITE OTHER FAMILIES WITH BABIES OVER TO PLAY.

Lie the babies down on the rug and watch them wiggle around and randomly grab each other's hands and maybe even notice one another's existence. Take photos. Grin at the other babies' parents. Drink coffee with the other babies' parents.

Sometimes the babies will cry or not be into it and that's okay too. No one will ever sympathize as perfectly with you when you have a crying baby as other parents of babies will. Make commiserating faces at one another and have some more coffee.

Sometimes it will even be a gloriously relaxed way to socialize with other adults while enjoying the cuteness of happy babies.

This will seem super counterintuitive if you've never had a baby before, but:

When they are an infant is actually the best time to do fun adult things with them.

TAKE THEM OUT TO RESTAURANTS. FLY ON AIRPLANES.

When they're tiny, they're lightweight and portable, and they can't locomote themselves, and they just sleep through everything most of the time anyway, so you might as well enjoy yourself a bit!

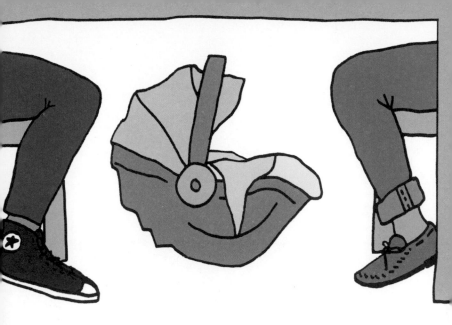

It's later on, when they're bigger and squirmier and more awake and opinionated about stuff, that things will be harder to do.

Think about it: Would you rather take a large meat-loaf to a restaurant, or a live chinchilla? There you go. That's the difference between taking a six-week-old and a six-month-old.

RATHER THAN A FREESTANDING, WHOLE-SEPARATE-PIECE-OF-FURNITURE TYPE HIGH CHAIR,

just get a small portable high chair seat that straps into a regular chair.

It takes up less space, is cheaper, and you can take it with you to restaurants too. Win, win, win.

PERHAPS THE NUMBER ONE THING YOU CAN SAY TO STRIKE TERROR INTO THE HEART OF A NEW PARENT IS: AIR TRAVEL.

Everyone's been on a plane with a crying baby or a freaking-out toddler at some point, and parents fear that they will someday be the ones on the plane with a crying baby or freaking-out toddler. But, with a few simple strategies, you can fly on a plane with a kid like a champ.

Tips for flying on planes:

Decide whether you will buy them a ticket

Up to age two your kid can fly ticketless as a "lap infant." This works great when they are actually an infant and you can basically just spend the whole flight holding them, feeding them, letting them nap, etc. Once they get bigger and squirmier it can be a bit trickier. Decide if you'd rather pop for their own seat (which they may or may not stay in) or, if there are two of you, if you're okay with them crawling all over your laps and the floor between you.

Keep them entertained

Babies will mostly be entertained by eating, and perhaps by a favorite toy. But as kids get bigger, entertainment becomes increasingly essential. You are officially allowed to throw whatever rules you may have at home about screen time out the window when you're on a plane. Get a pair of child's headphones to use with a tablet or the back-of-seat TV, if your flight has them. But include analog entertainment too; a book to read out loud and some coloring supplies are perfect. Also, an experienced-parent favorite is a roll of painter's tape. You can let your kid stick it all over everything—the seats, themselves—then just peel it off when you start your descent.

Deal with ear pressure

The most effective way to deal with painful ears during takeoff and landing is to suck on something. Luckily, babies already tend to do a lot of this, be it on bottle, boob, or pacifier. For older children, like with the screens, go ahead and break whatever rules about sugar you have and give them lollipops. They'll be thrilled (and you'll be relieved to know that the idea of the "sugar high" is, scientifically, largely a myth—kids get amped up at birthday parties by being around other kids and festivity, not because of the cake).

Mind your manners

While everyday rules about screens and sugar can be left behind with the ground, basic common courtesy and respect for our fellow human beings must remain. Do what you can to keep your kid from kicking the seats in front of them, banging the tray tables up and down, lolling in the aisles, touching other people, and so forth. In general, most of your fellow passengers will actually be very understanding of the fact that you're trying to manage a child-size ball of pure energy inside a metal tube packed full of bodies—and a basic level of respect goes a long way to keeping their good will.

When all else fails: resort to bribery

If your baby is just a baby who cries a lot, throw a bunch of earplugs and chocolates in your carry-on to hand out to your seatmates.

fig.1

fig.2

fig.3

When someone (usually someone without kids, someone with grown kids, someone super clueless, or someone who just has it in for you) gives your child a toy that makes loud noises, and you think the noises might actually drive you to the brink of madness:

Take out the batteries!

Your kid will happily play with it anyhow and never know the difference, and you won't be sent into a tizzy of aggravation every five seconds by beeping, blaring, or phrase-shouting voices.

Related bonus item: Hiding a toy away for a while makes it brand-new again!

When you start to feel anxious because your kid ate nothing but a big bowl of mashed potatoes, some cheese cubes, and four peas today, remember:

Look at what they eat over the course of a week, rather than in a day.

Nearly always, they'll self-regulate, gorging themselves on fruits or veggies one day to make up for that other day when they ate a third of a hot dog, a goldfish cracker, and a cookie.

The same goes for lots of other things too: Screen time, exercise, tantrums. If you look at patterns week by week rather than day by day, you'll have a much more realistic picture of what's actually going on with your kid, and be much less likely to freak out that they did a huge amount of this or that thing, or virtually none of this or that other thing, on a given day.

It's also worth noting: Some kids are big eaters and some are light eaters—that's just the way it is, and it's nothing to get worried about. All that emphasis placed on their weight when they're newborns can leave you feeling like their appetite or lack thereof is this great, big, important, dire thing. But really it's just one of the many ways that every kid is different.

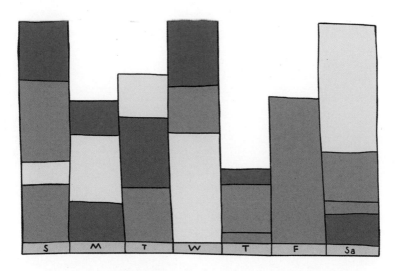

ODDS ARE VERY GOOD YOUR STANDARDS OF CLEANLINESS WILL GO DOWN ONCE YOU HAVE KIDS.

Scrubbing the grout in the bathroom may not seem like quite the priority it once did (if it ever did). Nor should it.

But there's one bit of housekeeping that can help you feel in control of your home and your life, rather than the other way around.

That can keep you from feeling like you're drowning under drifts of bath toys and burp cloths and onesies and incoming mail.

That can help you retrieve a bit of order from the chaos of existence.

TIDY.

At the end of the day do a quick sweep of the high-traffic areas of your house, grabbing everything you know has a place where it belongs and sticking it in that place. Your brain will thank you.

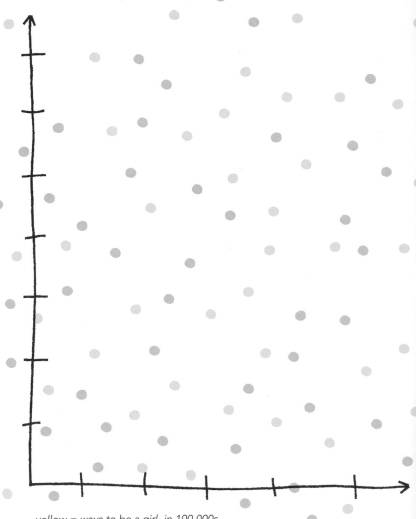

yellow = ways to be a girl, in 100,000s
green = ways to be a boy, in 100,000s

There are ten million ways to be a girl. And there are ten million ways to be a boy.

THIS APPLIES EQUALLY TO BOTH CHILDREN AND PARENTS.

Don't let anyone (not your dad, not a princess, not that kid on the school bus) tell you or your kid any different.

Sometimes you are really happy but you just don't know it yet.

ONLY LATER WILL YOU LOOK BACK AND, FROM A DISTANCE, BE ABLE TO SEE HOW HAPPY YOU WERE.

AND THAT'S OK.

The minor annoyances really are big when they're in your face right this very minute. But, with time, they'll fade away, and you'll be able to fondly remember those sleepless baby days or the chaotic birthday party or that mixed-bag family vacation.

Don't beat yourself up for not being able to relish every moment, in the moment. No one can. That's what the warm fuzzy glow of memory is for.

Take full advantage of things that make your life easier.

IF YOU CAN AFFORD GROCERY DELIVERY OR SOMEONE TO COME CLEAN THE HOUSE:

DO IT!

DO NOT FEEL GUILTY.

Now is exactly the time to utilize any and all tools at your disposal.

Bonus pro tip:

Use paper plates, cups, and napkins, and plastic utensils for the first few weeks of your baby's life. Throw them away after. Do not do dishes. The Earth will forgive you, just this once.

Bonus bonus tip:

Free two-day delivery on diapers is a thing that is readily available.

When you have a baby you're allowed to look like a total schlump.

You are also still capable of pulling yourself together and looking nice.

BOTH ARE FINE.

DO WHAT FEELS RIGHT IN THE MOMENT.

You can take a baby wherever you want.

IF PEOPLE DON'T LIKE IT, THEY CAN LUMP IT.

Babies are not inconveniences. They are human citizens of the world and, just like the rest of us, they get to go places.

Nice restaurant?	YES! ✓
Bowling alley?	YES! ✓
Sports bar?	YES! ✓
Airplane?	YES! ✓
Posh hotel?	YES! ✓
Library?	YES! ✓
Museum?	YES! ✓
Brunch?	YES! ✓
Birthday party?	YES! ✓
Swimsuit shopping?	YES! ✓

Everything
else

Love

The #1 thing a child needs, by a landslide, is love. The rest is frosting.

WHILE, YES, THERE IS A **LOT** OF OTHER STUFF INVOLVED IN RAISING A KID—A VERITABLE MOUNTAIN OF SUGARY PINK FROSTING—WITHOUT THE SOLID BASE OF LOVE—THE DELICIOUS, MOIST, AND CHOCOLATEY CAKE PART—IT'S NOT A CUPCAKE AT ALL.

Sometimes parenting will suck. That doesn't mean you're doing it wrong.

IN FACT, ALL IT MEANS IS THAT YOU ARE A LIVING, BREATHING, HUMAN PARENT RESIDING ON THE EARTH.

Experienced parents aren't kidding when they say there will be exquisite highs and abysmal lows. Both will come and there is almost nothing you can do about it.

Sleepless nights, temper tantrums, the tragedy of that first lost balloon. There will be plenty of times when your kids drive you up the wall, plenty of times when your heart breaks for them. And plenty, *plenty* of times when you are not the perfectly perfect parent you'd like to always be.

Negative feelings will happen. The only secret here is to do your very darndest not to take the negative feelings and transform them into self-loathing.

Ups and downs are inevitable when we cohabitate with and love another person. We all know this from romantic relationships. But somehow, when it's our child, we tend to kid ourselves into thinking that we should be skipping through a field of daisies with them all day every day, and that if we're not it means we're terrible at this.

You are not terrible at this. Your kid is a squirrelly human. You are also a squirrelly human. You will make it through just fine together.

Go outside.

Times to go outside:

- When you have a tiny baby and it will take you most of the day to gear up for a 15-minute walk around the block

- When you and/or your kid are feeling glum (you won't want to, but you'll almost for sure feel better once you do)

- When you and/or your kid are bouncing off the walls with excess energy (yep, even if it's raining—that's why they make rubber boots and umbrellas, and why warm dry pajamas and hot cocoa exist for when you come back inside)

- When your kid says they're bored

- When you are bored

- When it's a beautiful day

- When it's not a beautiful day (remember those rain boots!)

- When you realize you can't remember the last time you went and got any official "exercise"

- When you don't feel like doing the laundry

- When a treat is in order

- When you want to see nature

- When you want to see your neighborhood

Dress your baby however you want.

FOOTIE PAJAMAS ALL THE TIME OR FANCY OUTFITS EVERY DAY

CONFORMING OR NOT CONFORMING TO CONVENTIONAL GENDER NORMS

COZILY BUNDLED UP OR RELAXING IN JUST A DIAPER

Soon, your kid will be old enough to have an opinion about what sort of clothes go on their own body, but for now, you and you alone get to do the deciding.

And no one else gets to say squat about it (or if they do, you get to ignore them).

Pro tip: Babies don't actually need shoes. But, hey, if you can't resist the adorableness of tiny baby shoes, that's okay too.

People love to talk about how being a parent requires so much patience. Which can be worrisome if you're not in the habit of thinking of yourself as a particularly patient person. Like, uh-oh, you might think, I do not have the patience of a saint. Does that mean I'm going to be a bad parent? Nope!

If you don't think you have a lot of patience, just remember:

"Patience" is just the nice way of saying "stubbornness."

Sticking with something until it is done can look from the outside like one is being oh-so-wonderfully patient. When in fact, on the inside, you're just being stubborn.

Spending the whole weekend in the house until the child is at least sort of potty trained? Looks so patient! Feels so stubborn! At the end of the day (or the week, or the month) it's the same thing. Kiddo gets to be proud of those big-kid undies, and you get to stop changing diapers. It's a win for everyone. Who cares what was going on in your non-saintly soul in the meantime? You got the job done.

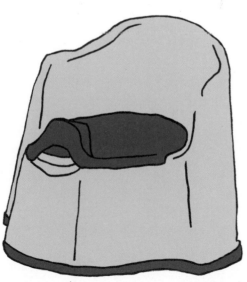

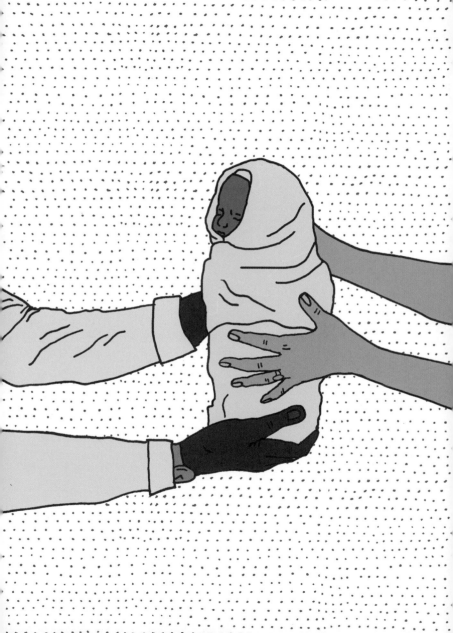

You deserve a partner in this.

Much of the time that partner will be your actual partner—husband, wife, boyfriend, girlfriend, etc.

But if you're a single parent, or if your life partner is not available for some reason (travels a lot for business, works the night shift, or whatever the particular circumstances of your own specific life together may be), you need someone else who's got your back.

One of your parents, a trusted friend, an awesome babysitter—find someone to give you the help and support you're entitled to.

Sometimes it really is just a phase.

Stages many kids enter and then emerge from pretty quickly:

One-year olds: attachment to one parent

Two-year olds: constantly asking "why?"

Three-year olds: tantrums

Four-year olds: being the life of the party

Five-year olds: extremely earnest mind-set

Six-year olds: sassy attitude

Some things are not a phase.

Your kid has their own identity. As time goes on, you'll come to recognize certain aspects of that identity that have been more or less consistent starting nearly from birth. It's pretty amazing to observe, actually.

Also not a phase:

Potty humor. That lasts a good decade or more. Sad but true.

Round-number ages (12 months, 2 years, 3 years, etc.) tend to be easy; half-year marks (18 months, 2½ years, 3½ years) tend to be hard. No one knows why. But it gets at what is perhaps the single greatest truth of being a parent:

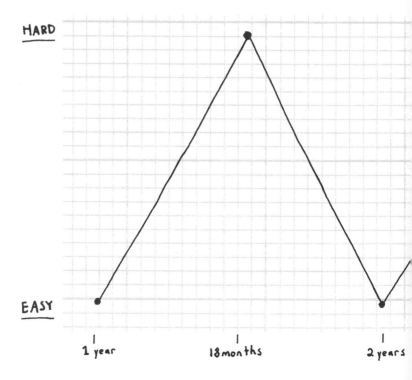

This too shall pass.

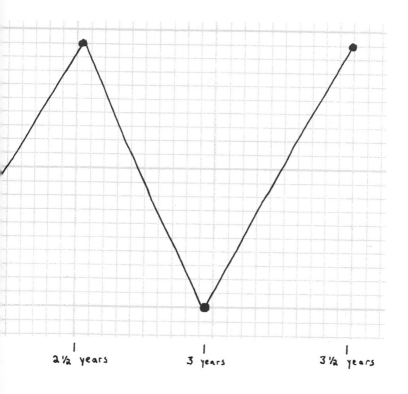

2 ½ years   3 years   3 ½ years

The number one tool in the parent-of-a-toddler toolbox:

 DISTRACTION

Oh look! A cloud shaped like a bunny!

Get used to getting rid of stuff.

When you buy something for a baby it seems as though the phase you're currently in will last forever, and you will need this thing forever. But in fact, most needs will be over almost before you know it.

Essential items will soon be obsolete.

That thing you couldn't live without will soon be the useless thing you find yourself tripping over.

Clothes that seem giant will be outgrown in a heartbeat.

FIND A SMALLER CHILD OR A GOOD CHARITY TO PASS THINGS ON TO SO YOU CAN GET THEM OUT OF YOUR HOUSE.

Stuff that will obsolesce:

- Strollers
- Car seats
- Cribs
- Changing supplies
- Nursing paraphernalia
- Baby bathtubs
- All clothing
- Virtually all baby blankets
- Nearly all toys
- Most books
- Potty training stuff
- Pacifiers
- Sippy cups
- Plastic plates and bowls and silverware

Stuff that won't:

- Beloved stuffed animals
- A special blanket or lovie
- A few forever books

ALSO: Hit up your friends with older kids for hand-me-downs.

MANY PEOPLE ASSOCIATE THE IDEA OF HAND-ME-DOWNS WITH BROWN 1970S FLARED CORDS AND <u>BRADY BUNCH</u> RAINBOW TEE SHIRTS. BUT IN FACT, OF COURSE, YOU'LL GET THE CUTE CLOTHES OF TODAY. AND THE CONCEPT'S JUST AS COOL AS IT WAS DECADES AGO.

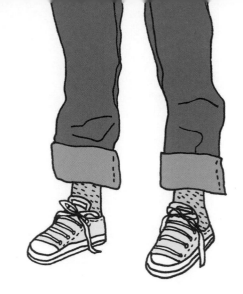

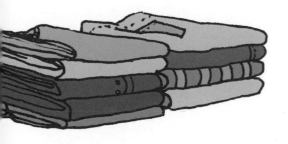

You may very well end up owning three car seats in your kid's lifetime.

This is just about as ridiculous as it sounds, but since it's how things very frequently wind up working out, you may as well accept it and move on with your life.

(And yep, this applies even if you don't happen to own a car.)

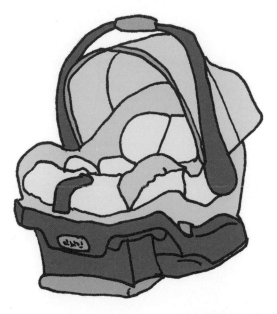

#1 INFANT SEAT

#2 REGULAR CAR SEAT

Nowadays most regular car seats are billed as "convertible"—meaning they can be configured to work for infants and booster-aged children as well. However, many new parents want the portability of an infant seat where the bucket with the baby in it snaps in and out of the car and can also snap in and out of a stroller and has a handle for carrying. And the day you get to replace the big, bulky, regular car seat with a slim little booster is a move towards flexibility that most don't want to pass up either.

While, usually with baby stuff, less is more, this is a case where many people don't want to opt for minimalism. As always, do what's best for you.

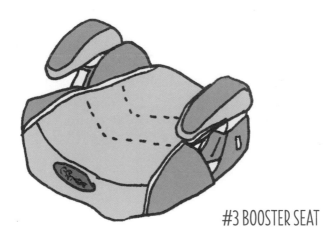

#3 BOOSTER SEAT

It's okay to take your messy toddler to a restaurant.

Just be sure to MASSIVELY overtip.

WHEN YOU WANT TO REWARD YOUR CHILD FOR SOMETHING—
GETTING DRESSED ON THEIR OWN, GOOD BEHAVIOR AT
GRANDMA'S HOUSE, SHARING NICELY, BRUSHING TEETH
WITHOUT LOSING THEIR MINDS, WHATEVER—

make time with you the reward.

Incentivize them with the prospect of their favorite outing or activity with you, or if an object or treat is the reward, make going and getting it together part of the fun.

Positive reinforcement + parent/kid bonding time! Win-win!

Knock knock.
Who's there?
Boo.
Boo who?
Oh no, why are you crying?!

What happens when it
rains cats and dogs?
*You might step in a
poodle.*

What's made of cement,
sits on top of a hill, and
howls at the moon?
*A coyote. The cement
was just to make it harder.*

Knock knock.
Who's there?
Interrupting cow.
Interrupting cow wh...
MOO!

Why don't fish play tennis?
*They don't want to get
caught in the net.*

What's a snake's
favorite school subject?
Hiss-tory

Two muffins were in the
oven. One turned to the
other and said, "It's hot in
here." The other shrieked,
"Ahhh, a talking muffin!"

How do you make a
handkerchief dance?
Put a little boogie in it.

What did the cherry with a stem say
to the cherry without a stem?
"Why don't you have a stem?"

Learn how to tell a joke and have a battery of kid-friendly jokes at the ready.

BEING ABLE TO CRACK YOUR KID UP IS NOT ONLY A WONDERFUL WAY TO CHEER THEM UP, DISTRACT THEM, OR CHANGE A BAD MOOD BUT IT ALSO GIVES YOU A CHANCE TO BE SILLY TOGETHER, BOND, PROMOTE CONFIDENCE, AND MAKE EACH OTHER LOOK WITTY.

People (especially people with bigger children or grown-up children)

really, really, really, REALLY want to hold the baby.

TAKE FULL ADVANTAGE.

Acknowledgments

Thank you to editor extraordinaire Deanne Katz for seeing the vision of this project so clearly from the beginning and guiding it so beautifully through to the end. Thank you to all the very fine folks at Chronicle including (but not limited to!) Brooke Johnson, Rachel Harrell, Freesia Blizard, Meghan Legg, Tamar Schwartz, Lesley Bruynesteyn, Marie Oishi, Lia Brown, Magnolia Molcan, Joyce Lin, and Cynthia Shannon. Thanks and high fives to Wynn Rankin for getting this whole crazy ball rolling. Deepest thanks to all my best parent pals who offered up their own tips and tricks to be included in this book: Shweta, Casey, Vanessa, Kate, Kristen, and Christina—you rock my world. Thank you to my own dear parents for ensuring I always knew that the cake part of my own personal page 92 cupcake was as vast as the universe. Thank you to Bill for being the best partner in this parenting gig that a girl could dream of. And most of all thanks to Mabel, for single-handedly teaching me nearly everything in this book, just by existing—you're my monkey and my shining star.